COPYRIGHTED MATERIAL

This book was made possible in partnership with:
Morgan H Jennings, Illustrator, and Cover Designer
Briana J Williamson, Formatting and Publishing, Publish With Me LLC

ISBN: 9798361839759
IMPRINT: INDEPENDENTLY PUBLISHED

This Book is Dedicated To:

My hero, Ruth (Auntie Ruthie) Williams.

She was the epitome of what love looks like. A lover of all children, she dedicated her life's work to caring for children especially those in foster care.

Thank you for teaching me how to love.
Thank you for loving my Kingston and Kaizen.
You are forever in my heart.
I love you.

Dezirai Jones

Hi! My Name is Kingston!

My mom says I'm made of cocoa beans, honey, and shea butter, (whatever that is).

I think she is only teasing.

HONEY

My friend Tommy who lives next door thinks our house always smells like chocolate chip cookies.

I tell him it's because my mom thinks our whole family is made out of chocolate.

Mama is in the kitchen stirring up brownie batter with her electric mixer.

Hey Mama!

Can I have a look?

Hmm so yummy and sweet!

COCOA

Yes, just like you my sweet melanin boy, says mama.

What's melanin mama?

Melanin is me and you son.

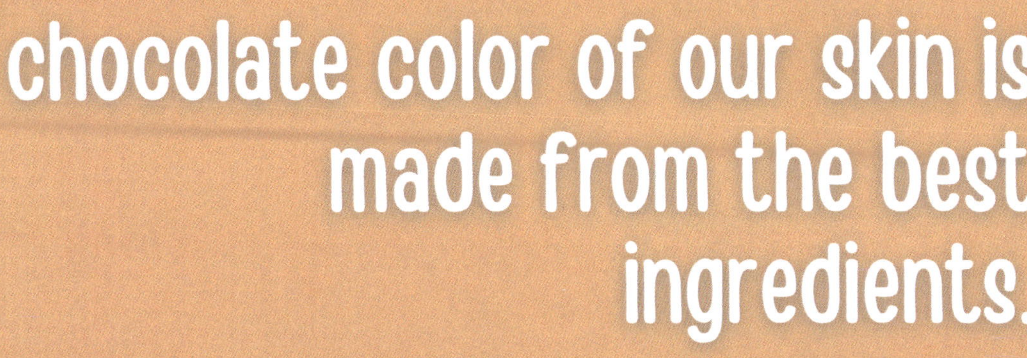

The chocolate color of our skin is made from the best ingredients.

You are special and sweet, always remember that.

Cocoa beans ✓
Honey and chocolate cake. ✓

I'll always remember that mama!

The next day at school,
Ms. Bettin asked the class to play a
game where we pick
out the dark colors in the
classroom.

Sally was the first to shout Gray!

Chris yelled out Blue!

Black Screamed Billie

Kingston! Karen shouted!

I am not a color, Kingston said.

Your skin is brown, Karen teased.

Karen says Ms. Bettin, "Apologize to Kington."

Class, you have a lesson to learn here, that was not a nice thing to say.

All people are different colors and shades.

Some shades are darker and others are lighter than others, but we still treat them all the same with care and respect.

My mom says my skin is melanin.
It's made of cocoa beans, honey, and chocolate cake.
I'm sweet and special. Kingston shared.

Hey! I want to be made of ice cream sandwiches and pop tarts shouted Jason.

Ooh, I'm sweet like cupcakes.
I'm a cupcake! Cierra hummed.

Class let's all draw pictures of the ingredients you're made of, says Ms. Bettin.

I ran off the school bus so excited to show mama my drawing! Look, mama! That's me! Yes, it is son!

It's melanin made.

For all the brown children around the world. Love who you are always.

Made in the USA
Middletown, DE
18 November 2022